MY NAME IS
SONI

My Conscience Writes Poetry

MY NAME IS
SONI

My Conscience Writes Poetry

Written & Published by Soni Kaur
London, UK

MY NAME IS SONI : My Conscience Writes Poetry
Written by Soni Kaur
Copyright © Soni Kaur 2022
Published in 2022
First published in the UK by Soni Kaur
www.sonikaur.co.uk

First edition

This paperback edition printed in 2022

A catalogue record for this book is available from the British Library

Paperback ISBN : 978-1-9163961-1-1

Printed and bound in the UK by Calverts
www.calverts.coop

Printed on Forest Stewardship Council® (FSC®) certified, elemental chlorine free (ECF), acid free paper, using Algae Ink™

ALGAE INK

The inside pages of this book are printed with Algae Ink™, an environmentally-friendly ink where the pigment component is bio-based, safe and renewable.

Living Ink, the company that produces Algae Ink™, based in Colorado, use by-product algae material grown at Earthrise® Nutritionals' farm, based in the Sonoran Desert.

The spirulina (a type of algae) grown on the farm remains 100% pure during its entire growth process as no pesticides, herbicides, preservatives, additives, genetically modified organisms (GMOs), stabilizers or irradiation are used.

As part of Earthrise® Nutritionals' ecological cultivation for Earth-friendly farming, there is no soil erosion or water contamination.

Spirulina is grown for a blue colourant called phycocyanin, which is extracted and used as a natural food colourant.

The remaining material is considered algae by-product which is transformed into small bio-based black pigment. These pigments are in the form of dry powder or liquid dispersion.

Algae is grown using sunlight, water, carbon dioxide from air and nutrients.

When algae grows, it absorbs carbon dioxide and produces oxygen.

Algae grows faster than terrestrial plants and are renewable.

Algae does not use traditional farmland, thus production does not displace food production.

At large-scale production, algae black pigments are carbon negative.

Algae Ink™ is the first commercially available ink with bio-based pigments.

Sources :
www.livingink.co
www.earthrise.com

(Grateful acknowledgement is made to Calverts for printing this book. Being a workers' cooperative, Calverts put into action cooperative values of and including solidarity, democracy and equality They also implement an environmental management system to reduce negative environmental impact.)

DEDICATIONS

Firstly, this book is dedicated to animals, the beautiful beings who truly and naturally understand the meaning and power of unconditional love

Animals are our greatest teachers and role models

I dedicate this book to all those beautiful brave strong souls who feel there is always hope, no matter what

The reality is, keeping the faith will get you out of the temporary darkness and into the light

This book is dedicated to all the strong fighters, the unconditional lovers and daring dreamers who believe in the beauty of life and who understand the power of today

It is dedicated to those who have faith and to those who are truthful and loyal to their purpose in life

To those who know they are changing the world every moment through their words and actions

To those brave enough to use the power of positive communication through their work and actions

This book is for you, the reader

I hope you enjoy the simplicity of this book
This book is especially for you
You did not find me
I found you

I managed to find my way to you through this book,
with the help of the universe

The messages in this book are especially for you

I hope you will be inspired in some way

I hope, after reading this book,
you try to become the best version of yourself

From the inner depths of my body, mind, soul
and heart, I express my unconditional love and
gratitude towards you, and the universe, for
leading me to you

THANK YOU

My mother and father
They took 9 months to create me
Every mother only wants the best for her child
I am where I am today thanks to
my Mother's silent prayers and blessings

My ancestors
Because of them, I exist today, here and now

My mentor and family
They taught me to be the best version of myself

Calverts in London (UK)
They printed my book

Living Ink in Colorado (USA)
They produce Algae Ink™

Earthrise® Nutritionals in California (USA)
They grow spirulina algae

Everyone who inspired me in my writing journey

To Mother Nature
For allowing me to take a natural resource from her
soils to manifest my passions, dreams, goals and
vision into physical reality, in the form of a book

To the universe and cosmos
I am grateful for everything
Thank you

MY AIM

I want to create a positive impact through my work,
writing and actions

I want to contribute towards
making this planet a better place

I believe that the world is
changed by example, not solely by opinions

I believe that leading by
positive example creates change

I believe actions create impact

Opinions alone do not
always have wings to create change

MY ROOTS

I am from the womb of a life creator
I am from the city of acceptance
I am from the state of forgiveness
I am from the country of unconditional love
I am from the world of miracles
I am from the Earth of Mother
I am from the universe of Father
I am from the galaxies of beauty
I am from the cosmos of atoms

LOVE IS WHAT I AM MADE OF

Integrity is my strength
Respect is my freedom
World unity is my family
Love is my every atom

Love is what I am made of

Therefore
I am,
Love

I AM

I am the sea of salty waters
I am the heavens of glory
I am the skies of depth
I am the rains of hope
I am the rays of bright light
I am the rainbow of luck
I am the soils of gratitude
I am the rainforests of the greens and the browns
I am the jungles of the lions and tigers
I am the atoms of the ether
I am the cosmos of infinity

DEEP

Just as the depth of the sea has no ending
The depth of my soul has no ending
The depth of my heart is endless
Anyone can seek

They will never find the seabed of my heart or soul

I am limitless
I am infinity

INSTINCT IS MY BEST FRIEND

Instinct is my best friend
Truth is my God
Humanity is my passion
Unconditional love is my religion

THE SUBSCRIPTION OF LIFE

When you are born
You are signed up to the subscription of life
The subscription fee is living a life full of purpose

Make the most of your subscription before it ends
Your time here on Earth is limited

Your time here on Earth will expire
when it is time for you to go

Only then will you receive
the full benefits of the subscription

The benefit of having lived a
fulfilled, purposeful and rewarding life

You must pay the subscription fees to
take advantage of the subscription

TODAY NEVER DIES

Yesterday never lies
Today never dies
Tomorrow never arrives

THE RIVER OF LIFE

Your health is a river of life
It never stops flowing
It always goes back to the source
The ocean of the cosmos

COSMIC MYSTERIES

A page of history in the book of your mind
The chapter of life rooted in your body

Your thoughts print
a new page of destiny every moment

The prophecies of the future
Living inside the womb of your instincts

The dream of a billion lifetimes
Ingrained in your soul

The sequel of lifetimes in your cosmic being
The cosmic mysteries of eternity

THE PROPHECY

Write your destiny with the pen of your mind

Your thoughts are the pen
Your soul is the ink
Your imagination is the paper

Words of destiny
Carved into the book of life
They become prophecies of fate
They promise your kismet

The pen that prophecises
Words of truth
Unfolds the prophecy of the enigma of life

But it is your belief that will write
your destiny onto the paper of reality

THE GODS OF MIRACLES

Let prayers from your mind be answered by the
Gods of miracles listening from the skies

They listen with the ears of their cosmic soul
The Gods of miracles know only miracles

Miracles of health
Miracles of happiness
Miracles of peace
Miracles of unity

Let your hands and actions of kindness
make a positive impact here on Earth

These are the miracles of you

Miracles of a helping hand
Miracles of smiles
Miracles of love
Miracles of joy

The Gods of miracles answer prayers
from the heavens of the skies

The people of miracles act through
actions of kindness from the lands of Earth

Let your hands and physical actions of kindness
make a positive impact here on Earth

JEWELS OF THE EARTH

Breathe in the winds of the Earth
that travel the seven seas

Eat mindfully the energy of the sun
that blesses every frozen mountain top

Drink the waters of the skies
that are sent from the Gods of rain

Roam the Earth of Mother and
let your feet kiss the soil with gratitude as you walk

Sleep under the open skies of the universe
Where the ancestors lay

Live in the life force of the magical ether

Appreciate the wisdom of the ones long gone
The ancestors of the universe

Burn every doubt and fear that you ever had
In the fire of freedom

VIBRATIONS OF THE EARTH

Listen to the vibrations of the Earth
Listen to Mother Earth
Listen to the messages
They communicate in silence
To the beat of your heart
To every cell of your brain
To every atom in your cell

SECRET WHISPERS OF THE EARTH

Listen to the whispers of the Earth
The echoes of wisdom
They travelled many generations
They travelled many dimensions
From ancestor to ancestor

The journey of countless souls
Of many unspoken words
Of a billion sunsets
Of millions of moon cycles
Of thousands of sea tides
Of infinity atoms

The rivers of the Earth know these secrets
The wind carries these whispers
Through the dancing desert dunes
Through the dense green forests
Through the innocent wild animals
Through the blessed waters of the Earth

The sun has been the witness
The greatest witness there has ever been
The long standing witness
When all else dies in season
The sun is still there

The seasons come and go
The roses bloom and wither
But the sun has always been there
Hiding behind the shadows of the moon
Holding back in the black of the night

Let the ears of your soul listen to these whispers
But it is only your heart that can understand them
It is only your soul which can appreciate them
It is only your lips that can whisper them
With the mouth of your conscience

Because your are the chosen one
The one who can understand
The one who will communicate the wisdom
To the unborn seeds of the future

BLESSED WATERS FROM
THE GODS OF THE SUN

At the top of the mountains
Where the sun first reaches its rays of light
The ice caps melt into icy waters
The water flows down the valleys
The journey is magical
The sparkling icy water travels towards Earth

A beautiful journey
The energized water finally reaches Earth
The Earth is grateful
The Earth drinks the water
The water nourishes the soils of Mother Earth
The water gives life and energy

Blessings from the Gods of the sun
flow down to you like this

THE WINDOW OF YOUR SOUL

Let the energy of the sun
enter through the window of your soul

Let the Gods of the sun
fill your entire being with energy

Let the dancing winds
caress every part of your body
with tender loving care

Let the rains of tears from the clouds
fill your soul with deep emotion

Let the rhythm of the Earth
fill your soul with ecstasy of vibrations

Let the space of the universe
surround your being like a temple of cosmos

MEET ME IN BETWEEN SUNRISE & SUNSET

In between sunrise and sunset
There is a place called today
They also call it here and now
This place gives me space to simply be

I will only ever meet you here
It is the place to be
There is no other place
This place is powerful

This
Here
Now

Meet me in between sunrise and sunset

Because

In between sunrise and sunset
There is a special place

The place where we dream
The place where we hope
The place where we pray

SUNNY LIFE

When you are upset
Life is a sunset

When you uprise
Life is a sunrise

BLUE SPACE

When the sun is ready to sleep
The dark goodnight skies wake up
The sun rests behind the veil of the night

When the sun is ready to wakeup
The dark goodnight skies go to sleep
The orange skies wakeup
They greet the sun as it wakes up

As soon as the sun is fully awake,
the blue skies are fully ready to
welcome the sun into their blue space

The sun has returned home after a few hours
sleeping behind the dark goodnight skies

The blue space is home of the sun

EAGLE WINGS

The mind can fly high

The wings of your mind are
more powerful than eagle wings

Spread the wings of your mind
Open the eyes of your mind

Take a trip to the cosmos
The eagle sees the Earth
You will see the whole universe

THE RIVER OF DREAMS

In the heat of the sun
My fears melt
They become a river of dreams
I flow to the source
I become one with the source
I become a fearless dream

I AM THE DREAM YOU FEARED

I am the rain you sought shelter from
I wanted to offer you my water

I am the leaves you shied away from
I wanted to offer you my food

I am the sun you were seeking shade from
I wanted to offer you my warmth

I am the thunder you hid from
I wanted to offer you my music

I am the wind you covered yourself from
I wanted to offer you my caressing touch

I am the lion you ran from
I wanted to offer you my courage

I am the dream you feared
I wanted to offer you your deepest wish

THE RIVER OF YOUR SOUL

In the darkest hours
Where fear breeds
Please know that fear is temporary

A temporary guest
A temporary perception
A temporary illusion

When sunlight reaches Earth
The cold ice of darkness melts

The warm water of hope
flows in the river of your soul

RAINDROPS OF HOPE

The raindrops of hope
They cry and wash the skies
They give hope to dry lands of Mother Earth

The sun rays of warmth
They heat the skies
They give energy to all life forms below

The soft clouds of beauty
They offer soft comfort
They kiss the skies with affection

SADNESS DOES SMILE

The sky was crying with rain from the pain

With each tear of rain
The forests were fed
The animals were watered
Nature was nourished

There is always a happy side to a sad story

THE GARDEN OF YOUR DREAMS

Nourish the garden of your dreams
Water your hopes
Nurture your vision
Look after your actions
Protect your beliefs under the shade
Care about the outcomes
Be consistent
Repetition and faith will manifest the results

FIERCE AS FIRE

Fierce as fire
Deep as the ocean
Calm like a mountain
Flowing like a river
Powerful like the sun
Peaceful like the skies

United and connected
Like all the rivers to the ocean

MY HEART VS THE OCEAN

My heart is like the ocean
The ocean holds water
My heart holds love

The water in the ocean is
deeper than you think

The love in my heart is
deeper than you will ever know

WE WILL GROW LIKE A TREE

Step into my heart
Our love will be a beautiful art
Come live in my heart

The rent is free
We will grow like a tree
The eyes of love will see

OCEAN OF BEAUTY

When you open your heart

It becomes easy to offer
your love unconditionally to all living beings

The love comes from
the depths of the ocean of your core being

You become an ocean of beauty
This beauty gives
Without expecting anything in return

By giving, you never become less or empty

This beauty is infinite and never ending

Never underestimate
the value and depth of this beauty

Never judge anyone who does not have the
desire to appreciate this natural ocean of beauty

Everyone has their own soul agenda and
are fighting their own battles

IN THE NAME OF UNCONDITIONAL LOVE

Endlessly beautiful
Truly dutiful
Intensely faithful
Deeply devotional
Love unconditional

IN THE EYES OF LOVE

In the eyes of love
Caring becomes natural
Unconditional love becomes principle
Rising becomes easy
The universe speaks
The secrets unveil themselves
The deepest mysteries unfold

INNER BEAUTY IS POWER

Passion is inspiration
Change is the evolution
Action is the movement
Inner beauty is power

SOW YOUR DREAMS

A seed of hope
A drop of faith
A ray of belief
A shade of prayer

MOON BEAUTY

Moon in the night sky
You stand in the cold
You stand in the dark
Still you give unconditionally

You offer your magical glowing light
You offer peaceful serenity to my heart
You embrace me with your beautiful face
You glow with beauty

You comfort me on dark nights
The sight of you calms my soul
Your presence brings feelings of happiness
I absorb the deeply powerful
glow of your moonlight

I can only repay you with a thanks
I can only repay with compliments
My compliments have no words

My compliments for you are
simply feelings of gratitude

SILENT INVISIBLE OFFERINGS

Reach out to people
Silently and unconditionally
Without them knowing

Through your prayers
Through your positive actions
Make a positive impact

Give without expectation
Give without reward of praise
The silent invisible reward will be beautiful

GIVER

Always be a giver
Be a giver of precious moments and memories
Giving time is the most expensive gift you can give

Time cannot be
Bought
Sold
Borrowed
Returned
Recovered

Give your time to those who need it the most
Be part of someone's beautiful memories
We only live once

GRATEFUL TAKER
BLESSED GIVER

When you take
Be a grateful taker
It is a blessing to receive

When you give
Be a blessed giver
It is an even bigger blessing to be able to give

Being able to give love, time and kindness
is a truly beautiful blessing

THE WELL OF LOVE

Only drink from the well of love
Only eat from the plate of knowledge
Only bite from the spoon of kindness

Take (burdens)
From the hands of the burdened
Give to the hands of the needy
Share with the hands of the humbleness

Only sleep in the bed of peace
Only love from the depth of the heart
Only act in the name of humanity

CHOOSE

Choose the journey of happiness
Choose the duty of serving others
Choose the deed of selfless service
Choose the passion of helping others
Choose the actions of kindness
Choose the words of inspiration

Choose the life of unconditional love and gratitude

Always

PEACE IS THE GLUE

Peace is the glue
that holds humanity together

Unconditional love is the bond
that holds relationships together

EAT A SPOON OF HAPPINESS

Eat a spoon of happiness
Bite a piece of joy
Drink a glass of humble
Breathe a breath of gratitude
Sleep a night of peace
Act a moment of kind
Give a life of unconditional love
Take a handful of wisdom
Be a human of humanity
Live a life of compassion

NECTAR OF HAPPINESS

Water you soul with the nectar of happiness
Feed your mind with the food of imagination
Soothe your heart with the music of silence

LOCK OF IGNORANCE

Open the lock of ignorance
on the door of your heart

Open the lock with the key of
unconditional love and gratitude

Entrance is by invitation
Only you can invite yourself

Self acceptance and
self unconditional love is the invitation

Once you unlock your heart,
you unlock your life

The password to life is
unconditional love and gratitude

YOUR BODY IS YOUR HOUSE ON EARTH

Nourish your body
It is the only part of you that will
house you here on Earth

Care about your mind
It is the tool that will help you progress

Love your soul
It is the only part of you that will
remain with you eternally

YOUR HEART IS YOUR FLAGSHIP GUIDE

Your five senses can deceive you with illusion
Let your heart guide you
Let your heart become the five senses
View the world with the eyes of your heart
Your heart can be your flagship guide
You will sense truth and purity

A CONVERSATION WITH INSTINCTS

Instincts always speak to you
The conversation is one way
Instincts do the speaking
You do the listening

The advice is always to help you
To progress forward and upwards
Towards your higher purpose

The more you listen, the more you trust
The louder the instincts become
Listen with the ears of your soul

RAISE YOURSELF UP

Regret pulls you backwards
Negativity pulls you downwards
Being humble keeps you centred
Hard work pushes you forward

Unconditional love and gratitude raises you up high

TODAY IS MY HUSBAND

I am married to the now of today
I am divorced from the future of tomorrow
I am widowed from the past of yesterday

TOMORROW IS A LIE

Yesterday is a memory
The past once was

Today is the truth
Here and now is the reality

Tomorrow is a lie
No one ever saw tomorrow

Just be here and now
That is all there is

THOUGHTS & ATOMS

I wonder
You wonder
We wonder

Where am I
Where are you
Where are we

I am together
You are together
We are together

We exist as one
Soul to soul
In another reality

Until the universe brings us together
Body to body
In the physical dimension

We wait patiently
We wonder curiously
We think deeply

We hope fiercely
We pray passionately
We dream infinitely

TRUE CONTRADICTIONS

Your mindset can influence your thoughts
Your thoughts can influence your mindset

Your perception can change your reality
Your reality can change your perception

Deep words have deeper meanings
Deep meanings have deeper words

Think about it

LIFE ON DIVERSION

Life diversions are the universe speaking to you

They may create undesired events and
inconvenient circumstances

They become omens and life lessons

These are the
unspoken words of universe communication

The universe is speaking to you
The universe is teaching you

The message is that there is something more
beautiful and promising waiting for you

The universe is diverting you to a different road

When life is on diversion
You will travel a new journey
On the road of healing and progress
This will prepare you for your new destination

The new road will lead you to a more beautiful life
Where destiny is waiting for you
At your new beautiful destination